# Anxiety Relief Coloring Book for Adults and Teens:

*100 Creative and Anti-Stress Coloring Designs to Soothe Anxiety | Featuring Mandala and Flowers Design for Calmness and Relaxation Mindfulness & Dreaming Flowers for Women*

If you enjoyed this coloring book, please consider leave us positive review ☺

Scan this QR Code to leave a review.

SCAN ME

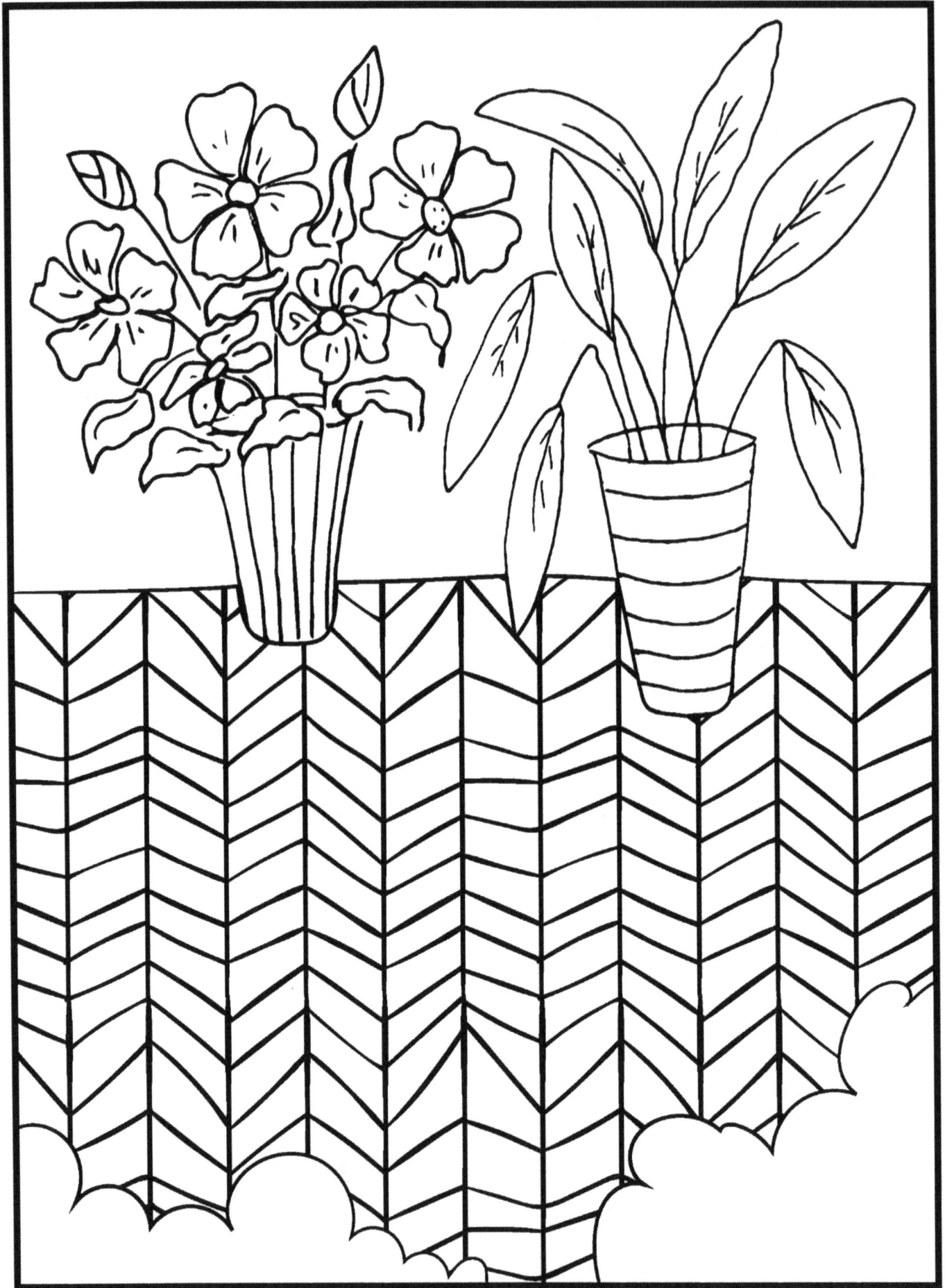

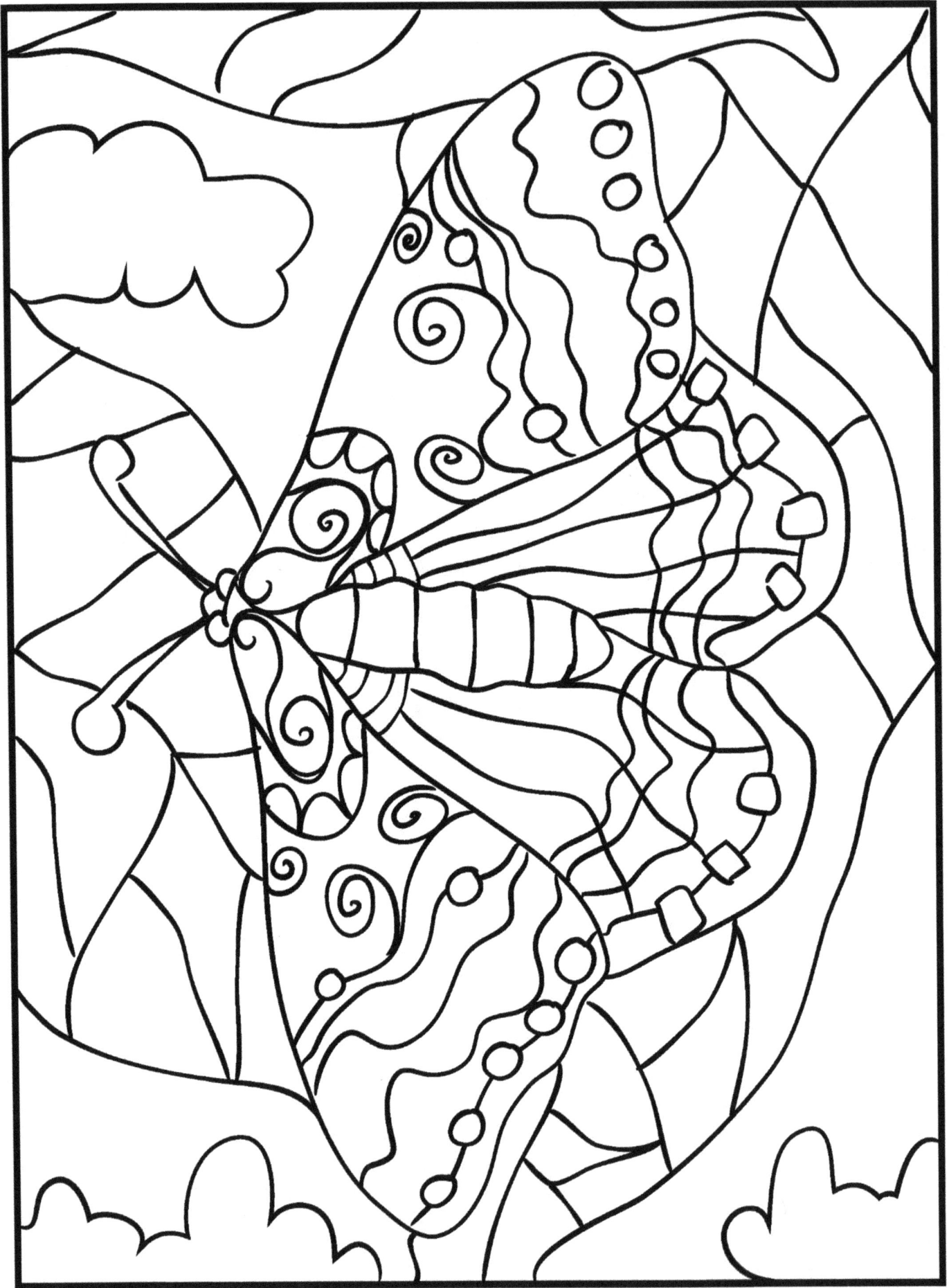

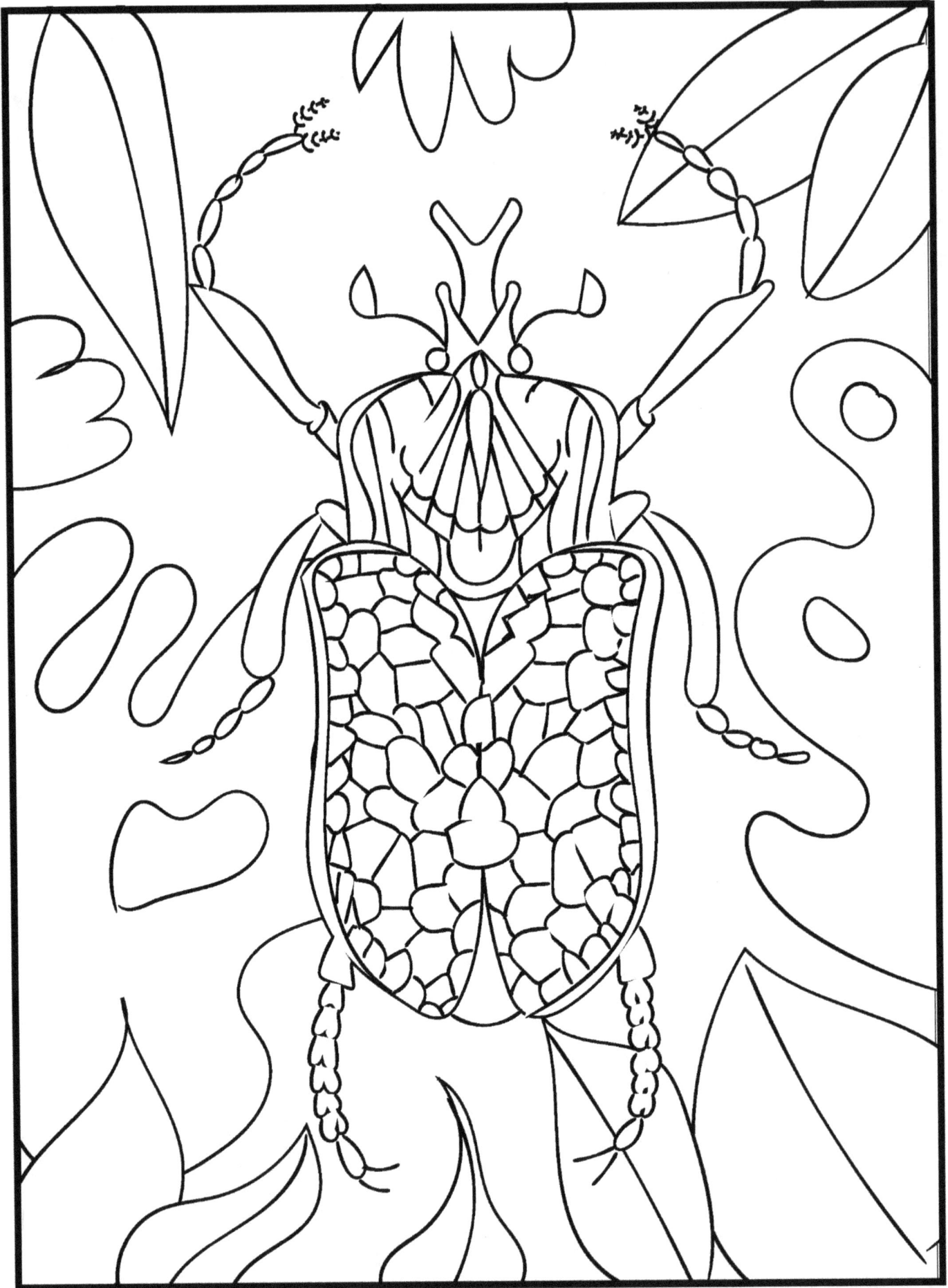

# Thank You

You could have picked from dozens of other books, but you picked our book.

**Anxiety Relief Coloring Book for Adults and Teens**

So, THANK YOU for getting this book and making it to the end.

Please consider posting a review on Amazon.

**Posting a positive review is the best and easiest way to support the work of independent authors like us.**

Your feedback will help me keep writing the kind of books that will help you get the desired results.

It can be something short and simple ☺

Scan this QR Code to leave a review.

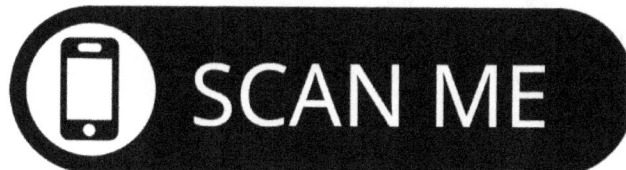

SCAN ME

www.ingramcontent.com/pod-product-compliance
Lightning Source LLC
Chambersburg PA
CBHW080518030426

42337CB00023B/4559